CREDIT RE

THE ULTIMATE GUIDE SYSTEM ON HOW TO REMOVE
NEGATIVE ITEMS FROM YOUR REPORT AND IMPROVE
YOUR SCORE WITH AN EASY PLAN

THE SECRETS TO RAPID RESTORE AND FAST RESULTS

Descrierea CIP a Bibliotecii Naţionale a României
PETERSON, CHARLES
    Credit repair : the ultimate guide system on how to remove negative
items from your report and improve your score with an easy plan : the
secrets to rapid restore and fast results / by Charles Peterson. - Bucureşti
: My Ebook, 2018
    ISBN 978-606-983-614-9

336

CREDIT REPAIR

THE ULTIMATE GUIDE SYSTEM ON HOW TO REMOVE
NEGATIVE ITEMS FROM YOUR REPORT AND IMPROVE
YOUR SCORE WITH AN EASY PLAN; THE SECRETS TO
RAPID RESTORE AND FAST RESULTS

My Ebook Publishing House
Bucharest, 2018

CONTENTS

INTRODUCTION

I want to thank and congratulate you for purchasing this book **"Credit Repair: The Ultimate Guide System On How To Remove Negative Items From Your Report And Improve Your Score With An Easy Plan; The Secrets To Rapid Restore And Fast Results"**

This book contains practical steps and strategies on how to thoroughly purge out negativity from your credit book as well as possible ways to manage to live above necessary means.

Taking care of your credit issue is less demanding when you know the reason for the problem. You'll have a less complicated time repairing your credit post-dispossession if you comprehend what made you abandon. What would you be able to have accomplished something unexpectedly? Maybe picked an alternative home loan?

Dealt with your cash better? Understanding why the abandonment happened can enable you to keep it from happening once more.

If you haven't been planning your salary, begin now. Having a financial plan isn't the errand numerous individuals think it is. At the point when done right, spending calms budgetary pressure since it causes you settle on choices about spending your cash. If you had a financial plan before the dispossession, however, didn't stick to it, you can begin once again. Keep in mind to include your "genuine spending" to your financial plan toward the finish of the month. Along these lines, you can see where you've overspent and made the fundamental spending changes.

Just sit back and fully grasp how you can take control over your life and finances as well without anyone being of significant assistance to you.

Once again, thanks for buying this book and I hope you enjoy it.

CHAPTER ONE

WHAT IS CREDIT REPAIR?

Credit repair is the procedure of settling poor credit footing that may have crumbled for a wide range of reasons. Revamping credit standing might be as essential as debating botches data with the credit organizations. Wholesale fraud and they harm brought about, may require extensive credit repair work. Another type of credit repair is to manage vital money-related issues, for example, budgeting and starts to address real worries concerning moneylenders

Various organizations asserting to do credit repair have jumped up after some time, and keeping in mind that some may give benefits that can help buyers, the real aftereffects of their endeavors might be addressed. Sometimes, credit repair may require legal and also monetary ability. Contingent upon the degree of the issue, it might need mainly tidying up misunderstandings, while in different cases proficient mediation is necessary.

In spite of the fact that various organizations guarantee they can tidy up terrible credit reports, rectifying incorrect data that may show up on credit reports requires some investment and exertion. The subtle elements referred to credit detailing offices can't be evacuated by an outsider. Or maybe the subtle elements, if distorted or incorrect, can be Disputed. Credit repair institutes may explore such data, yet so can the individual the report is surveying. People are qualified with the expectation of complimentary credit reports at regular intervals from credit announcing organizations, and also when an unfavorable move is made against them, for example, being turned down regarding credit in light of data in the report.

But what exactly is bad credit?

Bad credit portrays a past inability to stay aware of your credit assertions and the powerlessness to get affirmed for new credit. It implies you haven't paid your previous credit commitments on time, that is if you've paid them by any means.

Your credit account history is gathered by organizations called credit authorities (additionally alluded to as credit detailing offices) and accumulated into a credit report. Having bunches of negative data, late installments or advance default, on your credit report implies you have bad credit. You may have had accounts sent to a gathering office, charged high adjusts, recorded chapter 11 or had a vehicle repossessed. Bad credit commonly happens when you have different instances of these things in a brief timeframe. Some negative occasions just need to repeat once to make loan specialists careful about working with you. This incorporates stuff like insolvency, repossession, and abandonment.

CHAPTER TWO

THE TRUTH ABOUT CREDIT REPAIR AND THE SIGNIFICANCE TO OUR SOCIETY

It's hard to explore the present society with an awful credit considering the number of organizations that utilizes your credit to choose whether to work with you and to set your rates. Customers with a disturbed credit history regularly look for credit repair to enhance their confidence to have a less difficult time fiscally. Contracting a credit repair organization frequently appears as the best alternative, yet is regularly the minimum feasible decision.

As you explore credit repair and assess the best alternative for your credit, here are the most basic things to think about credit repair.

• *Shutting accounts won't help*

There's a great conviction that lone open records are incorporated into a man's credit report, that end a record will expel it from their credit report. It is quite heartbreaking to learn that you were credulous that you can spare your credit by shutting a record that is giving you issues, you are very much mistaken. However, closing a record can hurt your credit score.

Closing a record won't expel it from your credit report. Every one of the insights about the shut record will keep on being recorded on your credit report as announced by your creditors.

If the record is on favorable terms or can be brought over into grandstanding by making up for lost time with the past due adjust, leaving the record open can enable you to repair your credit. You'll require open, dynamic careers with a positive installment history to enhance your credit score. Opening new records with an awful credit score can be troublesome so restoring the records you as of now have open can be significantly more straightforward.

- **Credit repair is on your credit report, not your credit score**

When you're repairing your credit, you're attempting to enhance the data on your credit report. This is the thing that at last impacts whether you have excellent credit or poor credit and is the premise of your credit score.

Checking your credit report is the primary thing you ought to do when you're prepared to begin taking a shot at your credit. You can get a free duplicate of your credit report once per year from each of the significant credit agencies.

- ***You can do it without anyone's help***

Numerous folks imagine that lone credit repair organizations can enable repair to credit, however, indeed a credit repair organization can do nothing for you that you can't improve the situation yourself. There's a lot of data accessible in books and on the web that you can use to instruct yourself on how credit functions and what you can do to repair your particular credit.

Evacuating negative data, for instance, should be possible with methods like credit report Disputes, obligation approval, and pay for obliterating and bounty reports. A considerable lot of these are similar systems credit repair organizations use to get negative data expelled from your credit report. Doing it without anyone else's help spares you cash as well as gives you power and control over your particular credit history.

There might be different circumstances in the future that you have to enhance your credit and once you can do it all alone, you never need to get assistance from an organization.

Disputes may be acknowledged when deficient or mistaken data shows up on their credit reports. Beside amending such data, or getting deceitful exchanges on one's credit, remaking and repairing credit can lay all the more vigorously on credit use and credit movement.

The repayment history of the individual can be a noteworthy factor on their credit standing. Finding a way to ensure payments are up and coming or enhance the installment plan for outstanding credit can valuably influence their credit score. Besides, the measure of confidence displayed by the individual can likewise assume a part. For example, if an individual is currently utilizing significant bits of the credit accessible to them, regardless of whether they are keeping up least installments on time, the extent of the obligation they are conveying can contrarily influence their credit rates. The issue is that their liquidity might be compelled by the general liability against them. By taking measures to decrease their general obligation stack, they may see changes to their credit profile.

- ***Change your habits***

Numerous individuals experience credit repair – in the case of doing it without anyone else's help or procuring an organization – so they can get cash, for a home loan or car advance, for instance. There's nothing amiss with this. Numerous individuals, tragically, wind up back in a similar circumstance since they don't get dependable, winding up with more obligation than they can deal with and slip once again into habits of missing installments.

To make your good credit to last, you need to create habits that will keep up the high confidence. This implies acquiring just what you can sensibly stand to pay back (and possibly somewhat less).

With regards to creditworthiness, an extraordinary dependable guideline to recollect is to pay your bills on time without fail. Loan specialists and creditors need to realize that you've possessed the capacity to fulfill your budgetary duties on time inevitably. Like this, paying bills on time is critical, crucial conduct to build up at an opportune time."

- *Your credit score causes you to understand where your credit stands*

Regardless of whether you have excellent or terrible credit depends on the data in your credit report. Be that as it may, it's inflexible to take a gander at your credit report and tell whether your credit is excellent or terrible. That is the reason watching your credit score is helpful in credit repair. A low credit score demonstrates a poor credit history that necessities work. As your credit score enhances, it's an indication that your credit history is making strides.

Your credit score depends on five classes of data: installment history, a measure of obligation, the time of credit history, sorts of credit records, and late applications for credit. Enhancing your credit in each of these regions will help your credit score.

Utilizing free credit score aids will enable you to screen credit advance at no cost. When you agree to accept a credit checking administration, search for one that doesn't request a credit card. Something else, there's a shot you might be deciding to receive a free trial membership that will begin charging you every month until the point that you drop the administrations.

- ***Evacuating precise negative data is just too extreme***

As a matter of particular emphasis, Credit agencies are just lawfully committed to expelling incorrectly publicized data from your credit report. Regardless of whether those mistakes are sure or the contrary is no outcome. It's the reality the data is incorrect that enables you to expel it from your credit report, not that it's harmful.

At the point when precisely announced negative data harms your credit, it's harder to evaluate this data because the credit departments have the rights to report this information.

The trustworthiness of the credit scaffold relies upon credit agencies detailing all accurate data, even data that is negative.

There are a few procedures to evacuate precise negative data – like an accumulated obligation you candidly owe. These methodologies may take additional time and exertion than a fundamental credit report question. For these kinds of records obligation approval (for accumulation organizations), pay for erasing, and altruism erasure demands are the best choices.

• *Doing nothing may be a procedure*

Negative data won't remain on your credit report until the end of time. Most negative data will just stay on your credit report for a long time. There are a couple of exemptions, and unpaid expense liens can remain on your credit answer for up to 10 years. Unpaid debts can stay on your credit report through the state's statute of constraints for that kind of obligation.

As opposed to prevalent thinking, making a move on a negative record does not expand the credit stated time restraint. Along these lines, if you pay off a six-year-old obligation accumulation, for instance, it will, in any case, drop off your credit report after the seventh year.

- ***Credit repair organizations are recurrently untrustworthy***

Credit repair organizations complete an unusual activity of elevating their administrations to defenseless shoppers who need better credit. We don't entirely see how credit functions or how much impact they have on their particular credit scores.

Numerous credit repair organizations make elevated guarantees – frequently guarantees they can't satisfy – charge direct expenses and neglect to convey in their administrations. However, clients who are new to the law wouldn't understand they were being exploited until it's past the point of no return.

How to evaluate credit repair companies and their services online

When you search for "credit repair" the primary sections (under the promotions and any nearby organizations on a guide) you get are likely the most significant, most respectable specialists in credit repair online. We should assess some of those passages to decide if they are honest to goodness and experienced in credit repair and whether there are any credit repair trick warnings.

Keep in mind that even reputable credit repair organizations (just like some other organization) can have adverse surveys when clients don't comprehend that the credit repair process is to a significant degree tedious and that nobody can guarantee particular outcomes.

In the event that any section on your credit report is accurate blue and the data detailed can be confirmed precisely, at that point by law, it can't be expelled, clarifies Heath. Frequently credit repair organizations can challenge the data, and on the off chance that it can't be confirmed, the thing must be evacuated. However, clients may not comprehend that once the obligation is refreshed accurately and on the off chance that it is still inside the statue of restrictions for accumulations for your state, despite everything you owe the debt and it will in all likelihood be accounted for back to the credit agency the next month. Clients don't have the right desires when utilizing a credit repair organization which can prompt disappointment.

"A credit repair organization can enable you to enhance your credit answer to the point where your credit score is expanded, and you can have a few alternatives for credit accessible to you," clarifies Heath. "Be that as it may, it's not an overnight fix. It required some investment to get into the credit wreckage, and it might remove some an opportunity to get from it."

A Perfect Example?
Lexington Law Firm

Lexington Law is a full-benefit law office first and a pro in credit repair second and has been doing business for a long time. The site asserts that past customers have seen a normal of 10 things (where a similar situation expelled from each of the three credit authorities considers three expulsions), or 24% of starting negative things, are evacuated inside four months. There is no assurance of your outcomes because each credit report and financial circumstance is so exceedingly personal.

At Lexington Law, you will work with authorized lawyers and their paralegals that spend significant time in credit repair. Their sole occupation is to be comfortable with the buyer security statutes in play that identify with credit repair and to speak with the credit departments, the creditors, and the gathering organizations for your benefit as relevant to your one of a kind case until the point when you achieve a determination.

You can track your case and screen your outcomes all day, every day through the site and even a versatile application.

However, In recent years, the Federal Trade Commission has sought after many credit repair organizations who have infringed upon the law. These agencies are regularly required to pay substantial fines and now and again are prohibited from working together in the credit repair industry.

A couple of ciphers you're managing a shady credit repair organization:

✓ they ask you pay forthright before any administrations start, refer to a connection with the legislature or uncommon association with the credit authorities,

✓ guarantee a particular credit score, guarantee to erase precise data from your credit report, neglect to illuminate you of your entitlement to question data specifically with the credit agencies,

✓ or request that you forgo your rights under the Credit Repair Organizations Act.

Overnight outcomes shouldn't be expected

It requires investment to modify an awful credit history. Your credit score considers your latest credit history more altogether than more *spicy* things. A decent credit history commonly has a negligible number of negative passages and bunches of late positive credit data. A couple of long stretches of on-time installments is a positive development. However, it won't give you great credit immediately. Over the long haul and the negative data tumbles off or gets more seasoned, and you supplant it with positive data, you'll see your credit continuously progress.

Repairing poor credit requires some serious work, so it's vital to be quiet with the procedure. The measure of the time it takes can shift from individual to individual contingent upon the data on your credit report and how you're going about credit repair. You may see quick lifts when something is erased from your credit report.

Besides, your credit score may vacillate amid the credit repair process as the data in your credit report changes. Try not to be frightened by drops in your credit score.

CHAPTER THREE
IMPROVING YOUR CREDIT SCORE

Living with severe credit today is conceivable, yet it's extreme. Bad credit makes numerous things troublesome, unimaginable, or more costly. For instance, did you know insurance agencies frequently charge a higher loan fee for drivers that have bad credit scores? In case you're getting new utilities turned on in your name, the organization will check your credit to choose whether you should pay a security store. We as a whole realize that banks check credit scores before they give you a credit card or an advance. As years pass by, the rundown of organizations who check your credit will most likely develop rather than recoil.

Why Pursue Credit Repair?

Credit repair is necessary to sparing cash on protection, advances, and credit cards; however, that is not by any means the only motivation to repair your credit. A superior credit score opens up new work openings, even advancements and raises with your present manager. On the off chance that you long for beginning your own business or only need the security of knowing you can obtain cash when you need to, you should repair your credit shortly.

Do it without anyone else's help

You've most likely observed ads for credit repair. Possibly pragmatic credit repair signs in favor of the street. You don't need to employ an expert to settle your credit. Honestly, there is nothing a credit repair organization can do to enhance your confidence that you can't improve the situation yourself. Spare some cash and the issue of finding a legitimate group and repair your credit yourself.

Before fixing your credit, you need to realize what you have to adjust. Your credit report contains every one of the missteps you've made that have prompted lousy credit. Read through your credit answer to perceive what are the negative things influencing your credit score.

You're additionally qualified for a free credit report on the off chance that you've been turned down for credit on account of something on your credit report, in case you're as of now accepting government help, in case you're jobless and intending to search for work soon.

Paying for Your Credit Report

If you've officially spent your free credit reports during the current year, you can order your credit reports accurately from the credit agencies for an expense. The departments all offer a three-in-one credit report those rundowns every one of the three of your credit reports next to each other. The three-in-one credit report costs more than a single credit report, yet not as much as the consolidated cost of acquiring your credit reports.

Why Order Credit Reports?

Some of your creditors and banks may report just to one of the credit authorities. What's more, since credit agencies don't regularly share data, it's conceivable to have several data on each of your reports. Ordering every one of the three reports will give you an entire perspective of your credit history and let you repair your credit at all three departments rather than only one.

It's a smart thought to influence an additional duplicate of each report on the off chance that you do need to Disputes data. You can send the copy of your answer to the credit authority and keep a clone for yourself.

After receiving your credit reports, read them through. If you have an elongated credit history, your credit reports may be a few pages in length. Do whatever it takes not to get overpowered by all the data you're perusing. It's a ton to process, particularly in case you're checking your credit report out of the blue. Take as much time as is needed and survey your credit report more than a few days if you have to.

Perusing Your Credit Report

Get comfortable with the data contained in each of your credit reports. They'll all look fundamentally the same as, regardless of whether you've ordered them from various agencies. Each credit report contains your characteristic data, itemized history for each of your records, any things that have been recorded in broad daylight record like a chapter 11, and the request that have been completed to your credit report.

Choosing What Needs Repair

Here are the kinds of data you'll have to repair:

❖ Off base data, including accounts that aren't yours, installments that have been inaccurately balanced.

❖ Past due records that are late charged off, or have been sent to accumulations.

❖ Maximized accounts that are long overdue.

Employing different shading highlighters for each sort of data to help you effortlessly influence a credit to repair design. You'll adopt an alternate strategy for inaccurate data than you would for a past due record so utilizing various hues spare time re-perusing your credit report each time you're prepared to balance an installment.

Questioning on the web is regularly speedier and more straightforward, however, abandons you with no paper trail (you could take screen captures of your Disputes). A similar thing goes for making an argument about the telephone.

Sending your question through the standard mail has a few favorable circumstances. To begin with, you can likewise send confirmation that backings your question, for instance, a wiped out check indicating you make your installment on time. You can also keep a duplicate of the Disputes letter for your records. At last, if you send your Disputes using affirmed mail with return receipt asked for - which you should - you have confirmation of the time you submitted. This is vital because credit authorities have 30-45 days to explore and react to your Disputes.

Since you'll be sending numerous questions, you can keep a credit report Disputes format on your PC that you can alter the various items and several credit departments.

Sending Your Dispute

When you submit your Disputes, send additionally incorporate a duplicate of your credit report which you're questioning featured and a duplicate (not the first) of any confirmation you have that backings your question. If you don't send enough data about your Disputes, the credit agency can choose your question is negligible and decay to explore the issue or refresh your credit report. If your problem is real, the credit department will direct an examination, which is frequently as fundamental as inquiring as to whether the data is exact, and returned to you with a reaction.

c

You can likewise send your question straightforwardly to the bank or business which recorded the data on your credit report. They have the same legitimate commitment to explore your Disputes and expel wrong, inadequate, or unverifiable data from your credit report.

What Happens After a Dispute

On the off chance that the question is fruitful and your credit report is refreshed, the department will roll out the improvement, alarm the other credit agencies, and send you a refreshed duplicate of your credit report. Then again, if the thing isn't expelled from your credit report, your report will be stimulated to demonstrate that you've disputed the data and you'll be given a chance to add an original proclamation to your credit report. Personal explanations don't influence your credit score, however, provide further understanding to your question when a business physically survey your credit report.

Your installment history impacts your credit score than some other factor - it's 35% of your score to be correct. Since installment history is such a vast piece of your credit score, having a few past-due records on your credit report will fundamentally hurt your score. Dealing with these is urgent to credit repair. You will probably have all your past owing records revealed as "present" or if nothing else "paid."

Get present on accounts that are past due, yet not yet charged-off. A charge-off is one of the most noticeably lousy record statuses and happens once your installment is 180 days past due.

Records that are reprobate yet under 180 days past due can be spared from charged-off on the off chance that you pay the aggregate sum that is past due. Be careful, the further behind you are, the higher your make up for lost time installment will be. Contact your creditor soon to make sense of what you can do to get back current. They might to forgo a portion of the late punishments or spread the past due adjusts more than a couple of installments. Tell them you're restless to evade charge-off, however, require some assistance. Your creditor may even be eager to re-age your record to demonstrate your payments as present as opposed to the reprobate. However, you'll need to converse with your creditors to arrange.

Pay accounts that are as of now charged-off. You're as yet in charge of a charged-wobbly. As they get more established, charge-offs hurt your credit score less, in any case, the outstanding equalization will make it hard - and in some instances incomprehensible - to get endorsed for new credit and advances. Some portion of your credit repair must incorporate paying charge-offs.

Another alternative is to settle charge-offs for not as much as the first adjust if the creditor consents to acknowledge a settlement and cross out whatever is left of the obligation. The defrayal status will go on your credit report and remain for a long time. You might have the capacity to persuade the creditor to erase charge-off status from your credit report in return for installment. However, this isn't effortlessly done. The most critical thing is to pay your charge-off, and on the off chance that you can get a positive record status, it's a unique reward.

Deal with accumulation accounts. Records get sent to a gathering organization after they've been charged-off or fallen for a while. Indeed, even records that aren't typically recorded on your credit report can be sent to a gathering office and added to your credit.

Your way to deal with paying accumulations is much similar to that for charge-offs, you can spend all required funds and even endeavor to get compensation for erase simultaneously or you can settle the record for not as much as the money owed. The gathering will remain on your credit report for a long time in light of the first misconduct.

Bring High Account Balances below Your Limit

Your credit use – a proportion that thinks about your aggregate obligation to add up to credit – is the second most significant factor that influences your credit score. It's 30% of your score. The higher your regulations are, the more it harms your credit score. Having maximized credit cards costs valuable credit score focuses (also exorbitant over-the-restrain expenses). Bring maximized credit cards beneath as far as possible; at that point keep attempting to pay the parties off entirely. Your credit score reacts better to credit card adjusts that is under 30% of as far as possible, underneath 10% is perfect.

Advance Balances and Your Credit Score

Your advance adjusts additionally influence your credit score comparatively. The credit score figuring looks at your current advance progress adapt to the first advance sum. The nearer your progress conforms to the first amount you acquired, the more it harms your credit score. Concentrate first on paying down credit card changes because they have more effect on your credit score.

Past Due Accounts versus High Balances

You'll most likely have a restricted measure of cash to put toward credit repair every month. Thus, you'll need to organize where you spend your money. Concentrate first on accounts that are in threat of getting to be noticeably past due. Get whatever a number of these records present as could be allowed, ideally every one of them. At that point, chip away at cutting down your credit card adjusts. Third are those records that have just been charged-off or sent to a get-together organization.

CONCLUSION

Thank you once again for buying this book.

I hope this book satisfied your curiosity and anxiety as well as tactically meet your expectations concerning how well you can manage your credit score as well as repair it in case of bankruptcy.

However, these strategies outlined in this book will remain a theory unless you practice it and recurrently take hold of your life and finances

Finally, if you enjoyed this book, then I will like to ask you for a favor, would you be kind enough to leave a review for this book on Amazon? It will be greatly appreciated

Thank You and Goodluck

www.ingramcontent.com/pod-product-compliance
Lightning Source LLC
Chambersburg PA
CBHW071125210326
41519CB00020B/6417